CUTE ANIMALS FROM MODELING CLAY

by Martin Birch

THIS BOOK BELONGS TO

. . . .

Table of Contents

WHAT DO WE NEED

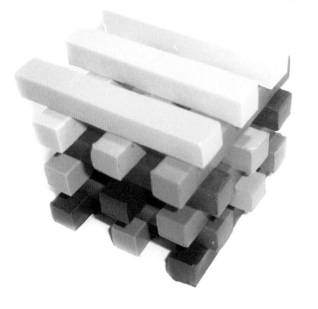

Obviously when we make figures we will need modeling clay. The best will be pack with color-full clay. As good as clay will be also modeling clay which will be great because we can indurate it with cooking.

To help with stick the clay great will be sharped tempered pencil. With it we can do holes with same size for example we do nose holes. As good will be empty pen's input. Let's start!

TECHNICS

1. From one part of modeling clay we make a little ball, with will be a basic figure when we will make animals.

2. The ball we roll and form to a shape of barrel.

3. When we knead and little roll a top part of ball we got a shape of water drop.

4. Next shape is kneaded to flat circle which also is made of ball.

5. Kneaded modeling clay circle we fold it for two half. In effect we receive a shape looks like "mouth".

6. Clay ball we roll to receive a long roller which we will need when we will make our figures.

DUCK

Body, head, wings, eyes, beak, fins

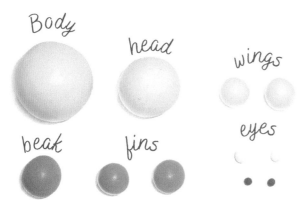

Body

head

wings

eyes

beak

fins

1. From clay we make eleven balls. One big for body, one in middle size for head and small for beak. We need also two balls for wings and two balls for fins. To make a eyes we need four balls, two bigger white and two smaller black.

2. Clay ball for body form to water drop shape. The same in wings but head we leave alone. Beak, fins and eyes we knead to flat.

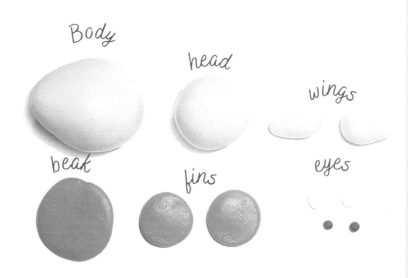

Body

head

wings

beak

fins

eyes

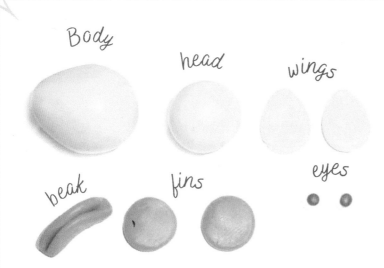

Body

head

wings

beak

fins

eyes

3. Formed wings we knead to flat. Beak we fold into halfs. Black circles we put on the white to make eyes.

4. We connect wings with body next eyes and beak with head. On fins we make a little cuts.

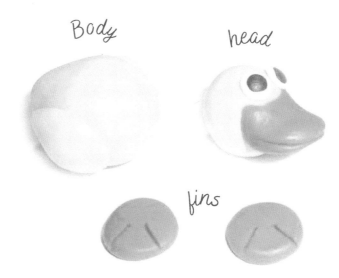

Body

head

fins

5. We connect head and fins with body. Also on a beak we make two little holes in effect you make nose. For better effect we explicit two little balls over the eyes.

PIG

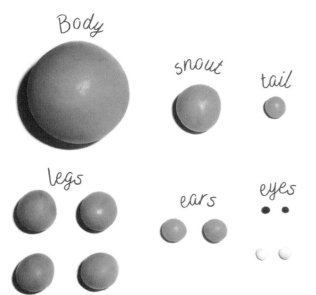

Body

snout

tail

legs

ears

eyes

1. From clay we make threeten balls. One big for body, One in middle size for snout and small for taill. Four in middle size for legs and four small for eyes. Two balls for ears.

2. We slightly roll body for a shape of barrel and snout knead for flat. We roll a tail from ball to long roller. Four legs and eyes knead for flat. Balls for ears form to water drop shape.

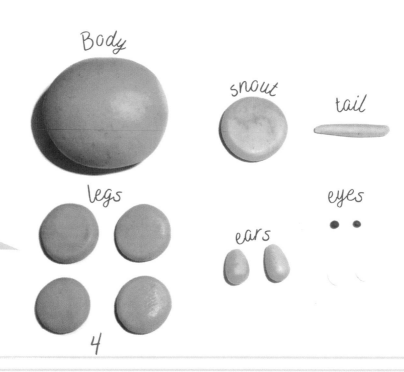

Body

snout

tail

legs

ears

eyes

4

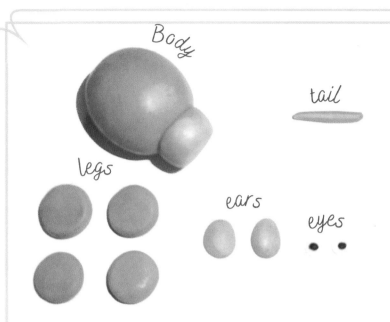

Body

legs

tail

ears

eyes

3. Kneaded ball of snout we connect with body, and black balls of eyes put on white. Ears formed to water drop shape and knead for flat.

4. On created body we put eyes and ears symmetrically.
Under body we put legs and fold tail to spring.

tail

5. Our pig is almost ready but it hasn't nose holes which we can do with a pencil.
For bonus you can make eyelids.

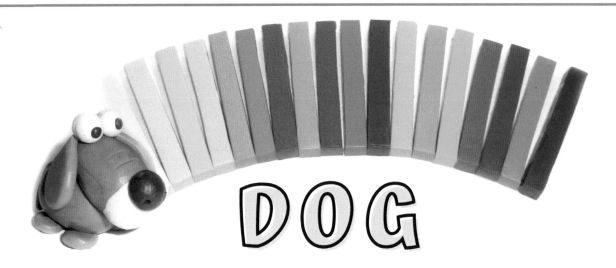

DOG

1. From clay we make seventeen balls. From small we make, tail, paws, eyelids, nose and eyes. From the balls in middle size we make head, mouth and ears. From big ball we make a body. Black very small balls we use it as eye element.

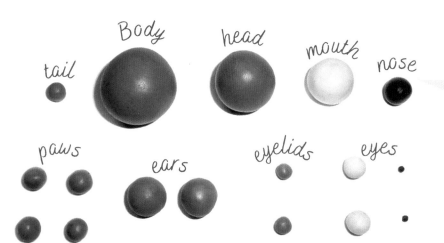

tail
Body
head
mouth
nose
paws
ears
eyelids
eyes

2. The tail we roll on long part. Body we form to barrel shaped. Head and ears form to water drop shape. And paws kneaded for flat.

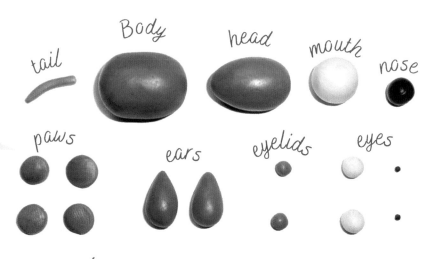

tail
Body
head
mouth
nose
paws
ears
eyelids
eyes

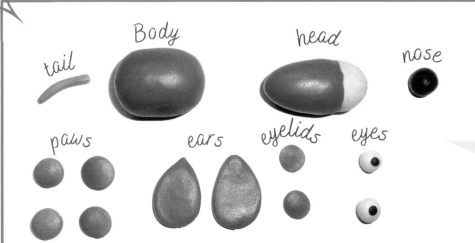

tail   Body   head   nose

paws   ears   eyelids   eyes

3. We connect head with mouth just like on picture. Ears and eyelids we knead to flat. Black balls of eyes put on white.

4. We put nose on head. We stick tail to body and paws connect with body too, but it have to be stability. We put eyelids on the back of eyes and connect.

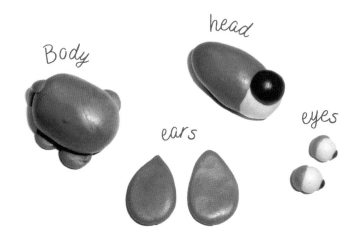

Body   head   ears   eyes

5. On the top of the head we put eyes and ears on sides. We put the head on body. In the end we make holes on nose and little cut to make mouth.

FROG

Body   head   front legs

back legs   eyelids   eyes

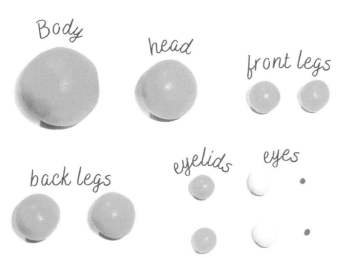

1.   From clay we make twelve balls. From big we will make a body, from balls in middle size we will make a head and back legs.
Little smaller we will use as front legs eyelids and eyes.

2. Clay balls of head and eyes we knead to flat.
Back and front legs we roll into rollers.

Body   head   front legs

back legs   eyelids   eyes

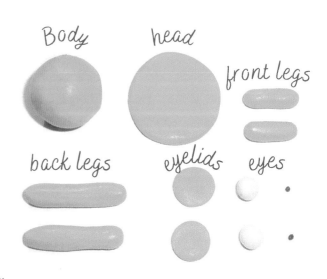

Body

head

front legs

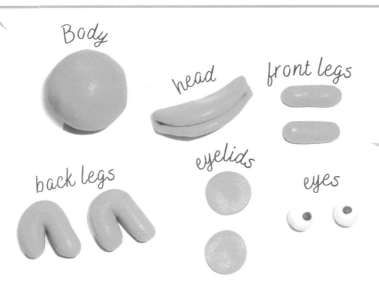

back legs

eyelids

eyes

3. Head we fold to two half and form lightly to receive happy mouth. Back legs fold in a half. Black balls of eyes put on white to receive frog eyes.

4. On next step we put the head on body and eyelids we stick evenly to eyes.

front legs

eyes

back legs

5. Froggy eyes we connect with head. Back legs we connect with sides of body and front legs we put on front of body. Next we make two more balls. We knead them for flat and connect with back legs and we recive fins.

fins

BEAR

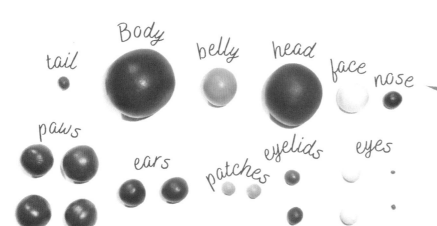

tail

Body

belly

head

face   nose

paws

ears

patches   eyelids   eyes

1. From clay we make twenty balls. Two big for body and head.
Eight in middle size 1- belly, 1-face, 4- paws and 2-ears. From ten small we will make tail, nose, patches on ears, eyes and eyelids.

2. After making all balls we knead for flat, belly, ears and eyes. Balls witch we use as paws we roll to receive rollers.

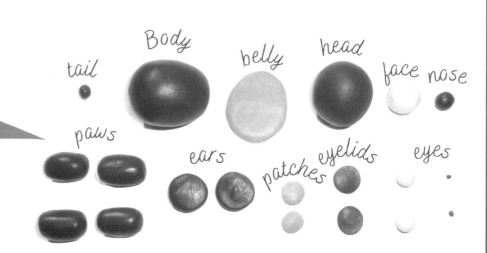

tail

Body

belly

head

face   nose

paws

ears

patches   eyelids   eyes

10

tail

Body

head

nose

paws

ears

eyelids eyes

3. Head we fold to two half and form lightly to receive happy mouth. Back legs fold in a half. Black balls of eyes put on white to receive frog eyes.

4. Ears we put on top part of head and connect it with body. Kneaded eyelids we connect with eyes.

Body

tail

nose

paws

eyes

5. We connect nose with face and eyes on head. We put paws on sides of trunk and we put tail on a back of trunk. On the end we make holes in nose by pencil. On paws we make claws by empty pen.

GIRAFFE

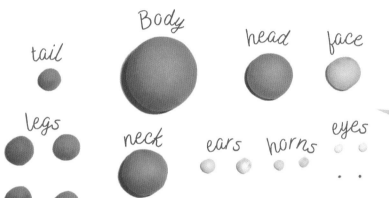

tail
Body
head
face
legs
neck
ears
horns
eyes

1. From clay we make seventeen balls. One big for body. Two in middle size for head and neck. Six smaller we use as tail, legs and face. Eight of the smallest we use for ears, horns and eyes.

2. Body we roll lightly to receive barrel shaped. Head we knead to receive egg. Legs and horns we roll to shape. We form ears to water drop shape and eyes we knead for flat.

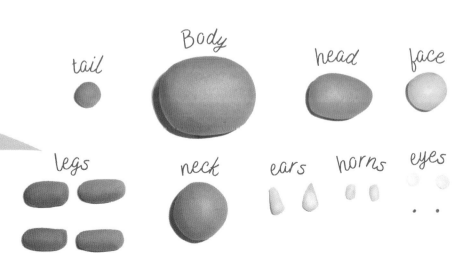

tail
Body
head
face
legs
neck
ears
horns
eyes

12

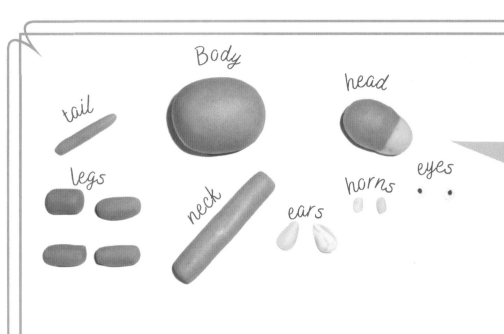

tail

Body

head

legs

neck

ears

horns

eyes

3. Tail and neck we roll into long rollers. We connect face with head and form to egg shape. Black balls of eyes put on white. Ears we knead to flat.

4. Legs connect with body to keep model balanced. We also connect tail with body. The eyes we put on the middle of head, ears on sides and horns on the top.

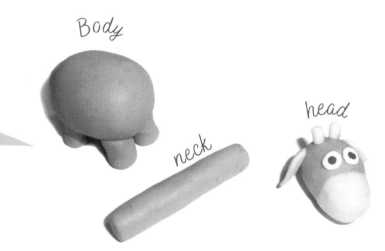

Body

neck

head

5. Next will be connect head with neck and neck with body. On face we make two holes to receive nose. Finally we make some small brown balls and knead them to make patches.

PENGUIN

Body

belly

wings

fins

beak

eyes

1. From clay we make eleven balls. One big for body, five in middle size to make belly, wings, and penguins fins. From smaller we make beak and from the smallest we make eyes.

2. The ball which will be belly we knead to flat. The body ball we roll to barrel shape. Wings, fins and beak we form to water drop shape. White balls of eyes we knead to flat.

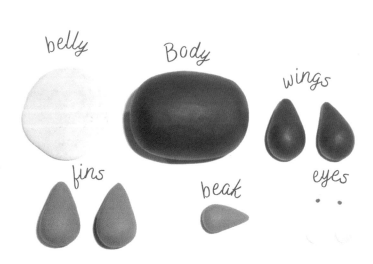

belly

Body

wings

fins

beak

eyes

14

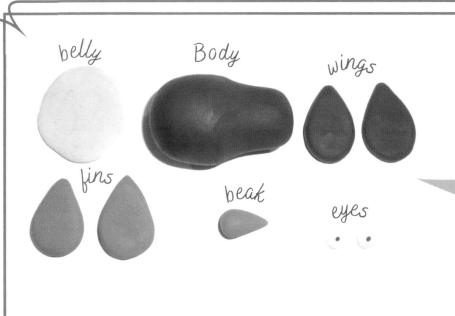

belly

Body

wings

fins

beak

eyes

3. Barrel body we have to roll more from a half of long. Wings and fins we knead to flat and black balls of eyes put on white.

4. The belly we stick together with body. On fins we make a little cuts, and connect wings with sides of trunk.

Body

fins

beak

eyes

5. Body we connect with fins. Beak and eyes we connect on the top of body. Finally we make little holes to receive nose.

MOUSE

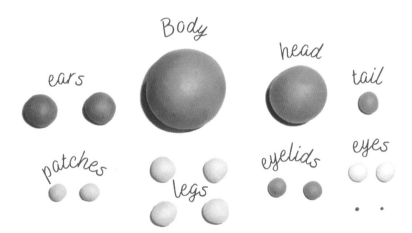

ears

Body

head

tail

patches

legs

eyelids

eyes

1. From clay we make seventeen balls. One big for body, a little smaller for head. From the balls in middle size we receive ears, tail and legs. From smaller we make patches for ears, eyes and eyelids.

2. Ears and their patches also legs we knead to flat. We roll body to barrel shape but head we form to water drop shape. We roll tail to long roller and black balls of eyes put on white.

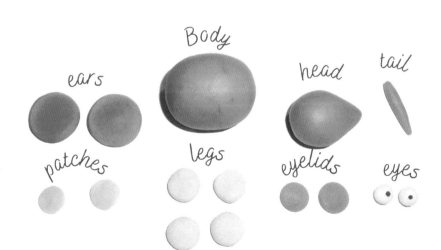

ears

Body

head

tail

patches

legs

eyelids

eyes

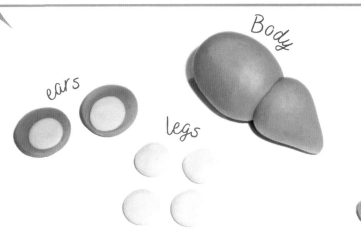

ears

legs

Body

tail

eyes

3. We connect trunk with head. And put patches on ears. Eyelids we put on back of eyes and stick them equally around.

4. We stick body together with legs. Ears we put on the top of a head and eyes on middle. Tail of mouse we connect on the backside of body.

5. On a mouse's face we make little spots. We make small cuts on a patches. From small ball we make nose and connect him with head.

nose

SNAIL

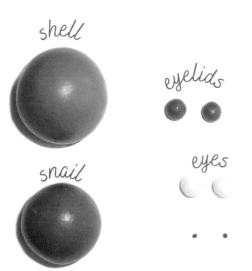

shell

eyelids

snail

eyes

1. To make a snail we need eight clay balls. Two big we will need to make shell and snail. From four small we make eyelids and eyes. We need to make two very small dark balls to receive snail's eyes.

2. Snail's home that is shell we roll to very long roller. We need the same to do with snail. Eyelids we knead to flat.

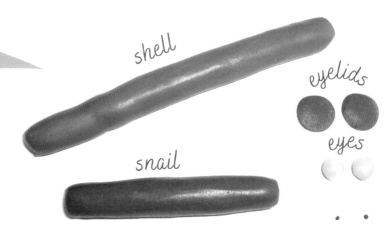

shell

snail

eyelids

eyes

18

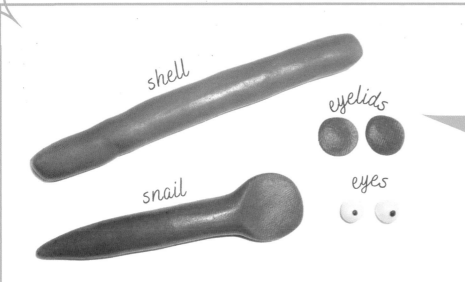

shell

eyelids

snail

eyes

3. One of ends of snail we roll a bit smaller to make tail but other side we knead to flat we receive spoon shaped snail. Black balls of eyes put on white and we receive snails eyes.

4. Our snail we fold to receive L-shape, then kneaded part we fold equally on halves to make face. Eyelids we put on back of eyes and stick equally around.

eyes

5. Shell we roll to make this shape which we put on a back.

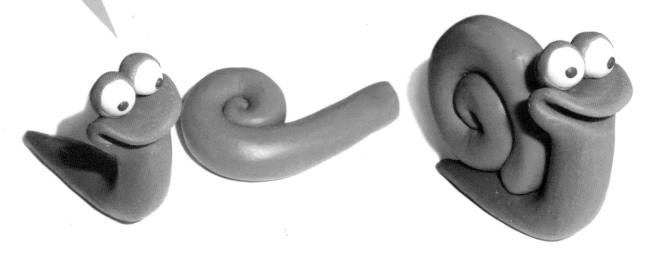

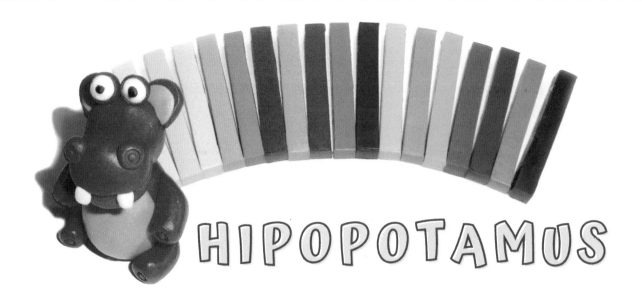

HIPOPOTAMUS

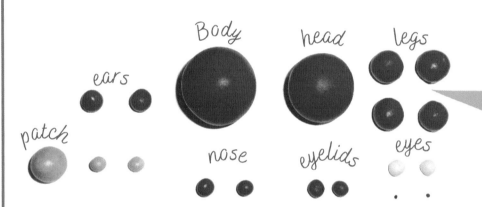

Body

head

legs

ears

patch

nose

eyelids

eyes

1. From mass we form 19 balls. Two big for body and head, balls of middle size for legs, and trunk patch, six small for ears, nose, eyes, and eyelids. At last two very small for eyes.

2. Body and head we form into barrel shape. Patches, eyelids and ears have to knead to flat. Legs we roll to rollers. Very small balls we put on the bigger eyeballs.

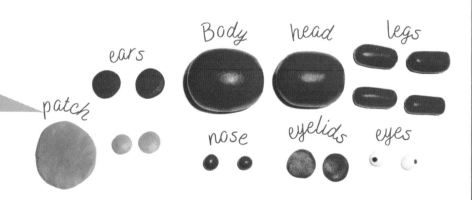

ears

patch

Body

head

legs

nose

eyelids

eyes

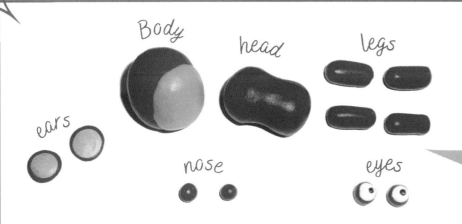

Body

head

legs

ears

nose

eyes

3. Keaded patches we put on ears and trunk. Eyelids we put on the backside of eyes and stick around. Head we roll in the middle with one finger to make 8 shape.

4. Nose balls we put on the front of head, on back we put eyes and ears.

Body

head

legs

5. We connect head with body. Legs we put on the sides. In nose and legs with we make small holes. At last we can make teeth for your hippo.

21

FISH

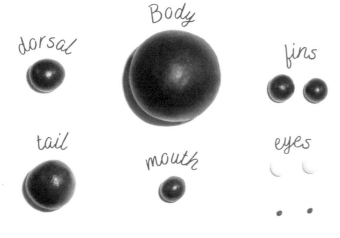

Body

dorsal

tail

mouth

fins

eyes

> 1. From mass we form 10 balls. One big for body, from middle size we need to make a tail, six small for mouth, eyes, dorsal fin and fins.

> 2. Fins and body we form into water drop shape. White eyeballs we kead to flat. Tail and dorsal fin we roll in thick rollers, however mouth we roll into thin, very long roller.

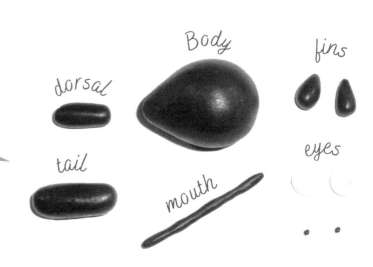

Body

dorsal

fins

tail

eyes

mouth

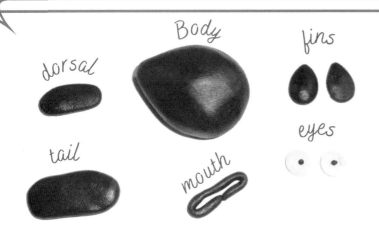

dorsal

Body

fins

tail

mouth

eyes

3. Dorsal fin and fins we knead to flat. Similarly we do with body but we knead only a little. Ends of mouth roller we connect like on a picture. Black eyeballs we put on the white ones.

4. Eyes we put on sides of body. Dorsal fin we put in the middle of the body and fit to it. Mouth we put in the front and fins on sides.

tail

Body

fins

5. Tail we form into arch and put on the back of body. We can also make some shallow cuts on fins by piece of carton.

CRAB

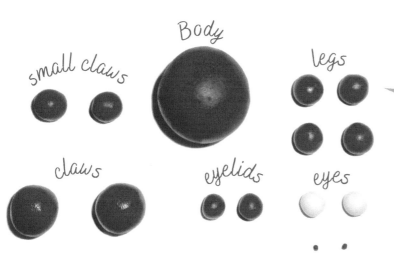

small claws

Body

legs

claws

eyelids

eyes

1. From clay we form 15 balls. One big for body. Two middle size for claws. Ten small for 4- legs, 2- eyelids, 2-eyes, 2- small claws. At last to very small black balls for eyes.

2. Legs and eyelids we knead to flat. Black eyeballs we put on white. Small and big claws we form into water drop shape.

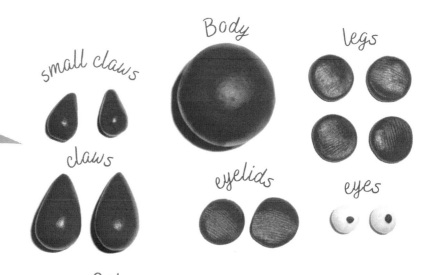

small claws

claws

Body

legs

eyelids

eyes

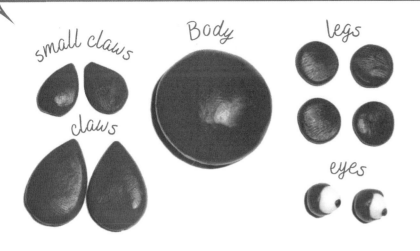

small claws

Body

legs

claws

eyes

3. Claws we knead to flat. Body also but only on one side. Eyelids we put on the backside of eyes and stick around.

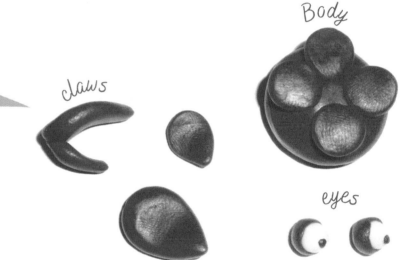

4. Legs we put on the flat side of body equally. Claws we form into light arch and put them together.

claws

Body

eyes

5. Claws we put on the front of trunk and eyes over the claws. We can also make two small holes to make nose.

TORTOISE

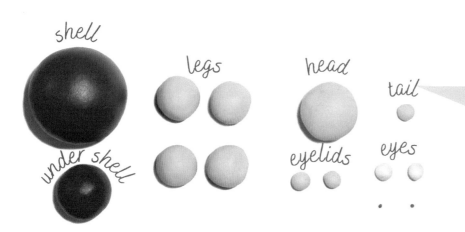

shell

legs

head

tail

under shell

eyelids

eyes

1. From clay we form 14 balls. One big for shell, two middle size for head and under shell, four a little smaller for legs, five small for tail, eyes, and eyelids. At last two very small for eyes.

2. Legs and tail we roll into roller. Head we form into water drop shape. Eyelids we knead to flat. Black eyeballs we put on the white ones. Undershell we roll into very long roller.

shell

legs

head

tail

under shell

eyelids

eyes

26

shell

legs

head

tail

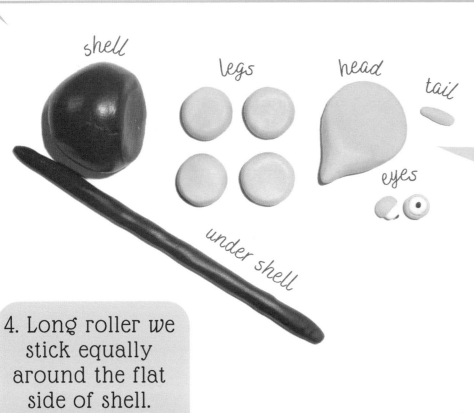

eyes

under shell

3. Legs we lightly knead. Shell we knead only on one side. Also head we knead to flat like on the picture. Eyelids we put on the backside of eyes and stick around.

4. Long roller we stick equally around the flat side of shell. Kneaded part of head we fold in half to make mouth. Tail we connect with shell.

legs

head

5. We connect legs with shell. We put eyes on head and connect it with shell. By pencil we make holes for nose.

CROCODILE

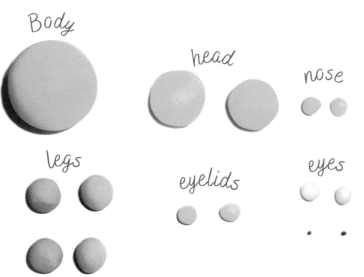

Body

head

nose

legs

eyelids

eyes

1. From clay we make 15 balls. One big for body, two in middle size for head, four a little smaller for legs and six small. 2- nose, 2- eyelids, 2 eyes and two very small for eyes.

2. Body and head we roll into water drop shape. In addition we roll body to make it longer. Eyelids and legs we knead to flat.

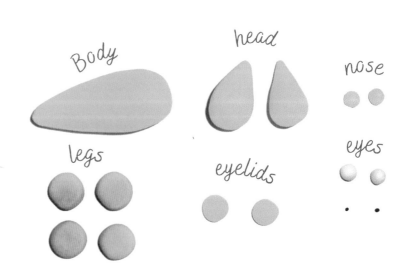

Body

head

nose

legs

eyelids

eyes

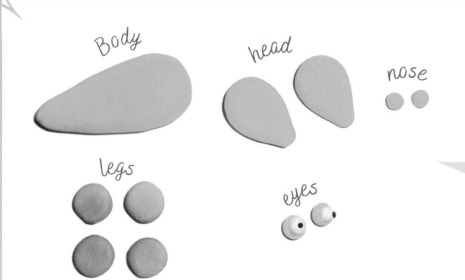

Body   head   nose

legs   eyes

3. Body and head we knead to flat, we put black balls on white. We stick eyelids around the eyes.

4. We connect legs with body, we also put head parts together.

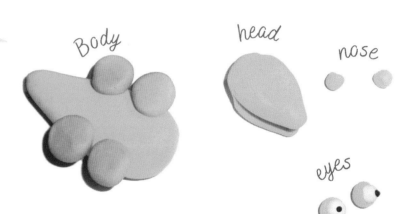

Body   head   nose

eyes

5. We put everything together. Head on front side of body. Eyes on backside of head, and nose on its front side. We can also make some shallow cuts on trunk and head with piece of cardboard.

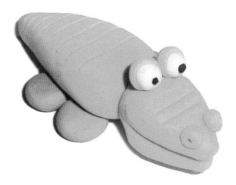

SEAL

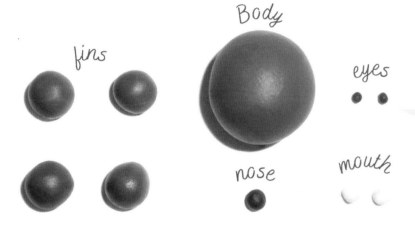

fins

Body

eyes

nose

mouth

1. From mass we make 9 balls. One big for body, four in middle size for fins. Three a little smaller, two for mouth and one for nose. Two very small for eyes.

2. Fins and body we form into water drop shape.

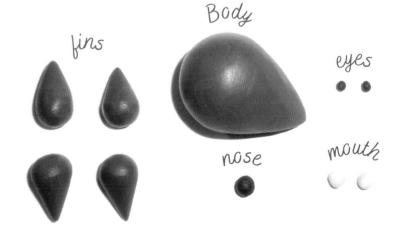

fins

Body

eyes

nose

mouth

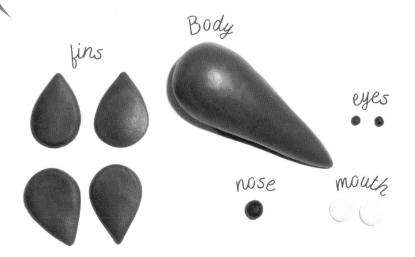

fins

Body

eyes

nose

mouth

3. Balls for mouth and fins we knead to flat. Body we roll to make it longer.

4. Two fins and body we fold into L-shape.

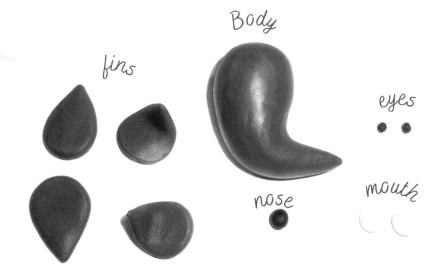

fins

Body

eyes

nose

mouth

5. L-shape fins we connect with front side of body and flat fins on back side. Mouth we put on "head" and nose a little higher. On top we put eyes.

ELEPHANT

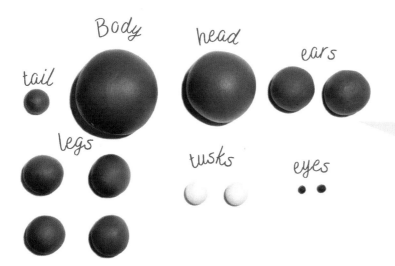

tail

Body

legs

head

ears

tusks

eyes

1. From mass we make 13 balls, one big for body, a little smaller for head. Six in middle size, 2-ears 4- legs. Three smaller 2- tusks, 1- tail, two small for eyes.

2. Head, ears and tusks, we form into water drop shape. Body we roll to receive barrel shaped. Similarly we do with legs we roll them into small rollers. Tail we roll into long roller.

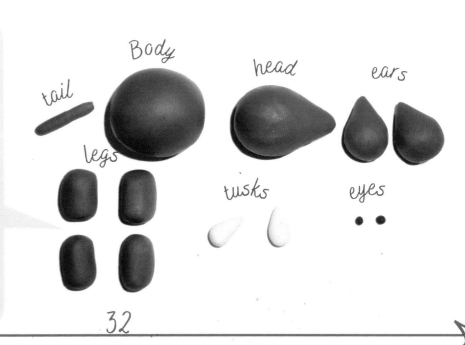

tail

Body

legs

head

ears

tusks

eyes

32

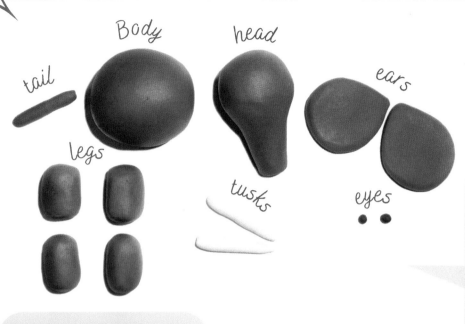

tail

Body

head

ears

legs

tusks

eyes

3. We knead ears to flat. We roll tusks to receive sharply ended rollers. We roll head like in the picture to receive shape.

4. We put legs and tail on body. Tusks we fold into L-shape. Ears we connect with sides of head and eyes on the front.

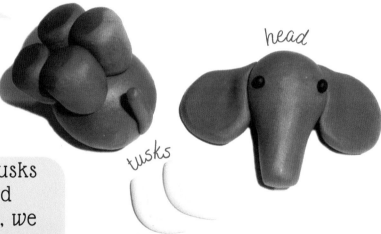

head

tusks

5. We connect tusks with head and head with body, we can also make some shallow cuts on head.

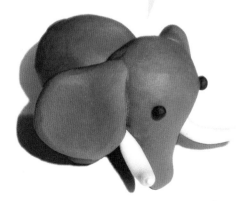

GORILLA

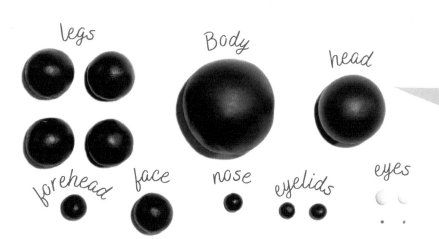

legs

Body

head

forehead face nose eyelids eyes

1. From mass we make 15 balls, one big for body and one in middle size for head. Five smaller for legs and face. Six much smaller for 2-eyes, 2-eyelids one for forehead and one for nose. At last two very small for eyes.

2. Legs and body we form into water drop shape, head and face we roll to receive barrel shape. Eyelids we knead to flat. Forehead we roll into roller.
Black eyeballs we put on white.

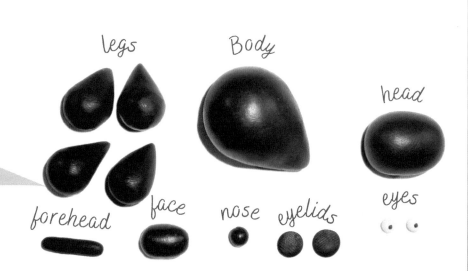

legs

Body

head

forehead face nose eyelids eyes

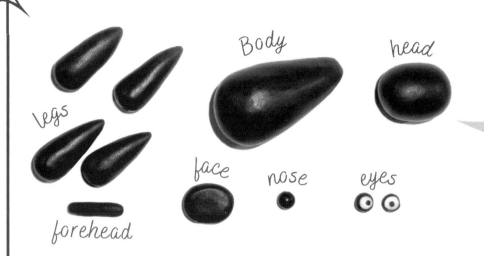

legs

Body

head

face   nose   eyes

forehead

3. Legs and body we roll lightly to make them longer. Face we knead to flat. Eyelids we stick around the eyes.

4. Body we fold into L-shape. We connect face with head. Over face we put eyes and between them we put nose.

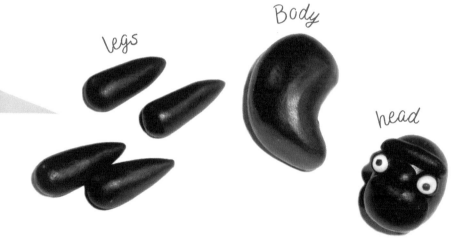

legs

Body

head

5. Received head we put on body in wider place. On front side we put legs vertically and on backside horizontally. At last we make some shallow holes in nose and shallow cut on face.

MONKEY

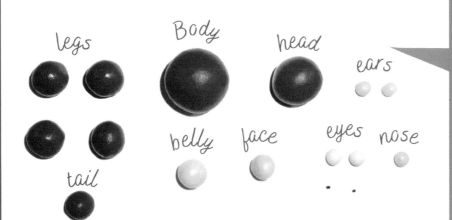

legs

Body

head

ears

belly

face

eyes

nose

tail

1. From clay we make 16 balls, one big for body, one a little smaller for head, seven in middle size 4-legs, 1-tail, 1-face, 1-belly, five small 2-eyes, 2-ears, 1-nose, at last two very small for eyes.

2. Legs and tail we roll into long rollers. Body we form into water drop shape. Ears and belly we knead to flat. Face we roll lightly. Half of head we knead to flat. Black balls for eyes we put on black.

legs

Body

head

ears

belly

face

eyes

nose

tail

legs Body head ears

face nose

3. End of legs we knead to flat. On body we put, on front belly and on back tail. Face we knead to flat. Eyes we put on the kneaded part of head.

4. Two legs we lightly fold into arch, second pair we fold the kneaded part into L-shape. We stick face to head, on it we put nose and over face we put eyes. On top we put on ears.

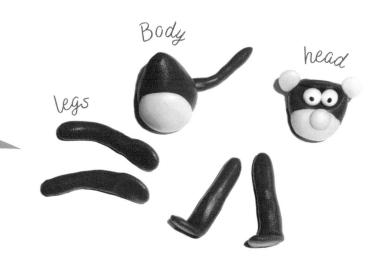

Body head legs

5. On body we put completed head and on sides we put legs like on the picture. With pencil we make small holes in nose and ears. With piece of cardboard we cut mass to make mouth.

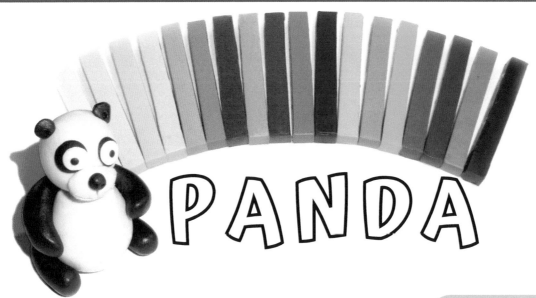

PANDA

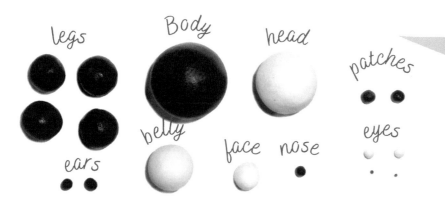

legs

Body

head

patches

belly

face   nose

eyes

ears

1. From mass we make 17 balls. One big for body and one smaller for head. Five in middle size, 4-legs, 1-belly. Smaller ball for face, seven small 2-ears, 2-eyes, 2-patches, 1-nose. Also 2 very small for eyes.

legs

Body

head

patches

belly

face   nose

eyes

ears

2. Legs we roll into long rollers. Body we form into water drop shape. Belly, patches, white eyes and ears we knead to flat.

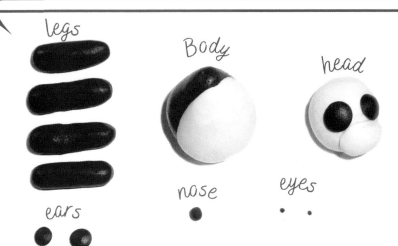

legs

Body

head

nose

eyes

ears

3. Belly we put on body. On head where should be eyes we stick patches, and under we put face. We put black balls for eyes to white.

4. On head where are patches we put eyes, on face we stick nose, on top of the head we put ears.

legs

5. We put legs on sides of body. At last we can make smile with little cut on face with piece of cardboard.

CAT

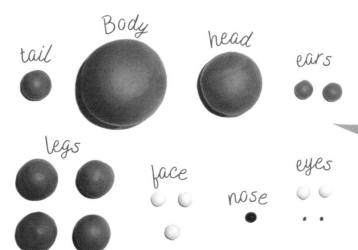

tail
Body
head
ears
legs
face
nose
eyes

1. From clay w make 17 balls, one big for body, one smaller for head, four in middle size for legs and one a little smaller for tail. Eight small balls 3-face, 1-nose, 2-ears, 2- eyes. Two very small for eyes.

2. Tail and legs we roll into long rollers. Body and ears we form into water drop shape. Balls for face we knead to flat. Similarly we do with eyes.

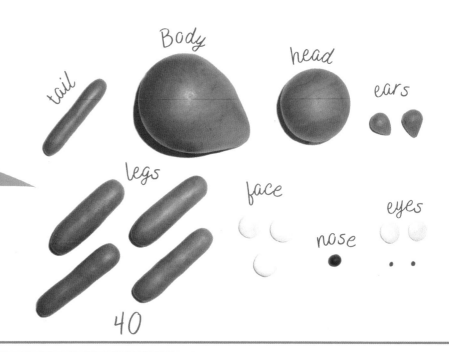

tail
Body
head
ears
legs
face
nose
eyes

40

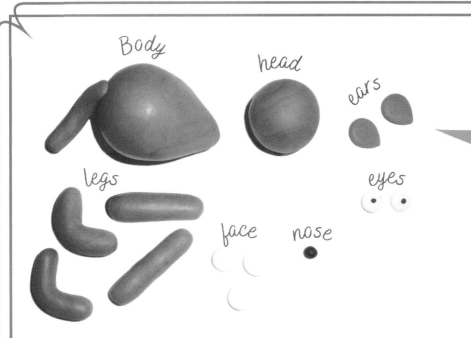

Body head ears legs eyes face nose

3. We connect eyeballs. Tail we stick to back side of body. Ears we knead to flat. Two legs we form into L-shape.

4. We put L-shape legs near place where should be head, second pair we put near tail. No the top of head we put ears. A little down we put eyes, in the middle we stick nose. Down we stick face.

5. Completed head we put on body. In the end we can make eyelids and make some holes for mustache with pencil.

RABBIT

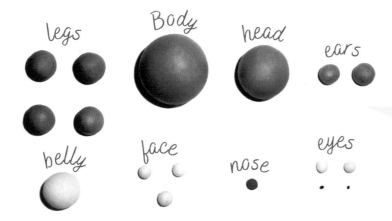

legs

Body

head

ears

belly

face

nose

eyes

1. From mass we make 17 balls. One big for body, one smaller for head, five in middle size 4-legs and 1-belly. Two smaller for ears. Six small, 3-face, 1-nose, 2-eyes. Two very small for eyes.

2. Legs and body we form into water drop shape, ears we roll into long rollers. Belly, white eyes and face we knead to flat.

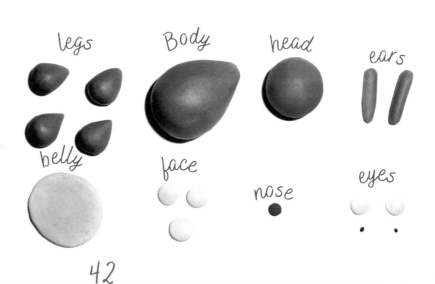

legs

Body

head

ears

belly

face

nose

eyes

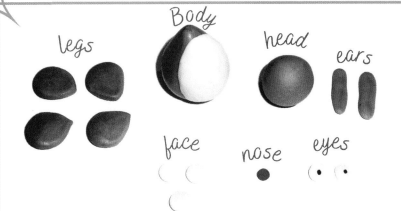

legs

Body

head

ears

face

nose

eyes

3. Legs we knead to flat and similarly we do with ears. On body we put belly and we stick it equally. We connect the eyes parts.

4. On sides and downside we put legs. On head we put face and nose.

Body

head

ears

eyes

5. On top of the head we put ears. A little down we put eyes. In the end we can make teeth, and with pencil make some rabbit mustache.

Download gift ebook

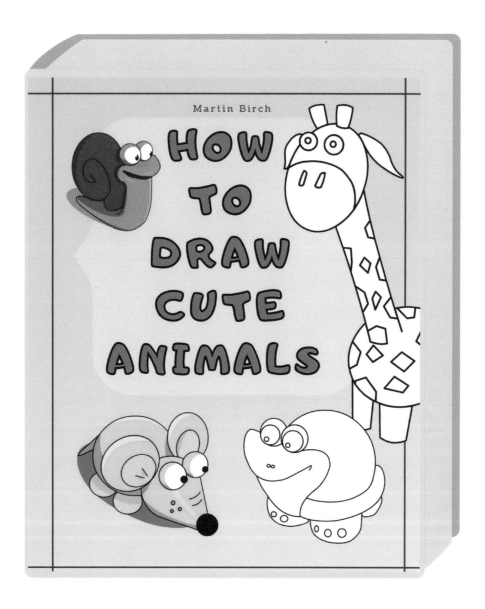

Scan QR cod

Printed in Great Britain
by Amazon

25932116R00030